Zebra caterpillar

Pipe-vine caterp...

DATE DUE		
APR 25 2011		
NOV 25 2011		

...ulphur caterpillar

American Painted Lady cater pillar

10-02
17. 00

Becoming Butterflies

by Anne Rockwell

pictures by Megan Halsey

Walker & Company
New York

One day Miss Dana brought a surprise to school—
three striped caterpillars and a flowerpot.
A green plant called a milkweed was growing in the flowerpot.

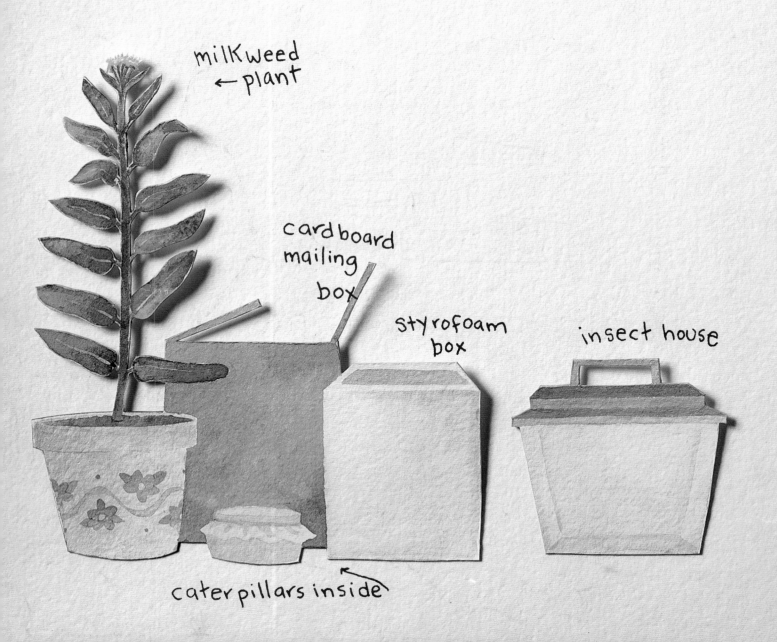

milkweed
← plant

cardboard
mailing
box

styrofoam
box

insect house

caterpillars inside

She told us butterflies don't have baby butterflies.
They lay eggs that hatch into tiny caterpillars.
The caterpillars eat and eat and eat
until it's time for them to become butterflies.
"You'll see," she said, as Julianna and I helped her
put the caterpillars in a box.

A tiny caterpillar

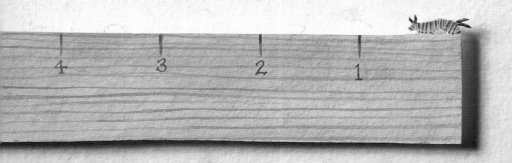

We put some milkweed in the box,
and our caterpillars started to eat it.
We put a screened lid over the top of the box
so they could get fresh air, but couldn't crawl away.
Then we drew pictures of them eating the milkweed.

The caterpillar
eats a milkweed leaf.

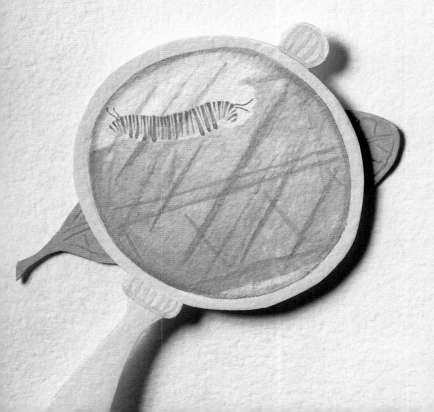

Our caterpillars ate and ate, and got bigger and bigger.
"But they're not becoming butterflies," Julianna said.
"They're just big, fat caterpillars."
"Wait and see," said Miss Dana.

A big, fat
caterpillar

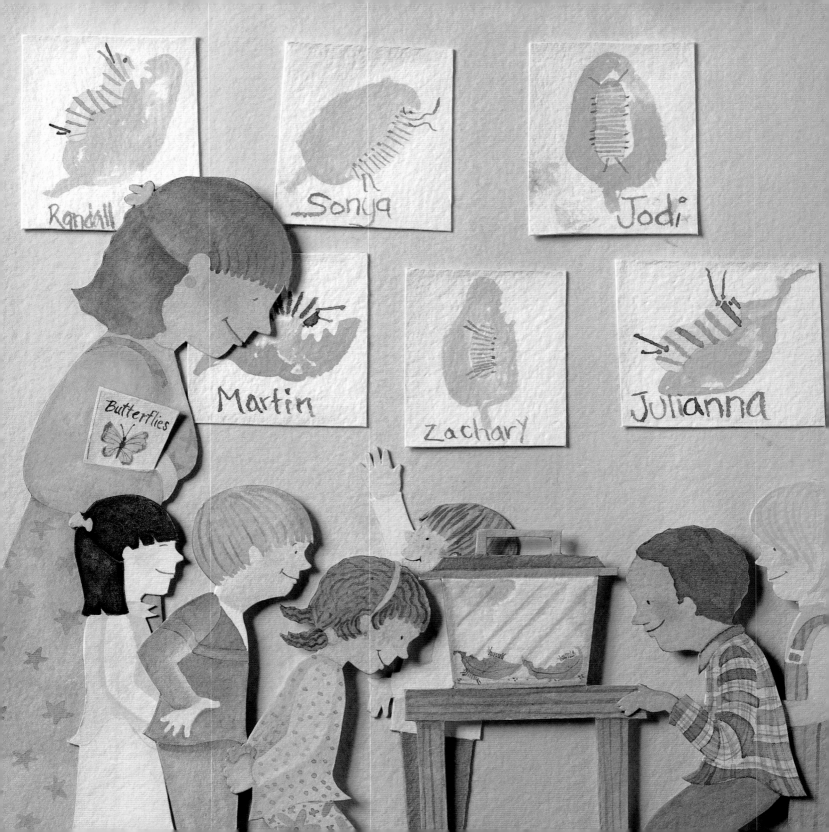

Randall

Sonya

Jodi

Butterflies

Martin

Zachary

Julianna

After three days our caterpillars got so big their skin split.
A new striped skin just the right size was underneath it.
I think caterpillars are always hungry
because ours ate their old skins and then more milkweed.
I drew a picture of that.

The
caterpillar's skin

A few days later, their skins split again.
When our caterpillars were about two weeks old
one hung upside down from the screened lid
from a little thread of black silk it made.
"Hey, look! It's spelling my name!" Julianna said.
She was right.
The caterpillar had made itself into the letter J.

The caterpillar
hangs upside down.

J

Soon that caterpillar's skin split,
but we didn't see any new striped skin.
All we saw was a glob of greenish-white jelly.
There wasn't a caterpillar to eat the old skin.
"Ick!" said Julianna. "It looks sort of sick!"
"It's not," Miss Dana said. "Watch what happens."

The caterpillar turns
into a chrysalis.

Ick!

We watched the jelly get smoother and greener.
Soon it was hard and smooth with a ring of gold dots.
"Hey! Now it's not icky at all," said Julianna.
"It looks like a beautiful jewel."
"But where did the caterpillar go?" I asked.
"It's becoming a butterfly," said Miss Dana.
"But first it must become a chrysalis.
That's what it is now."

The
new chrysalis

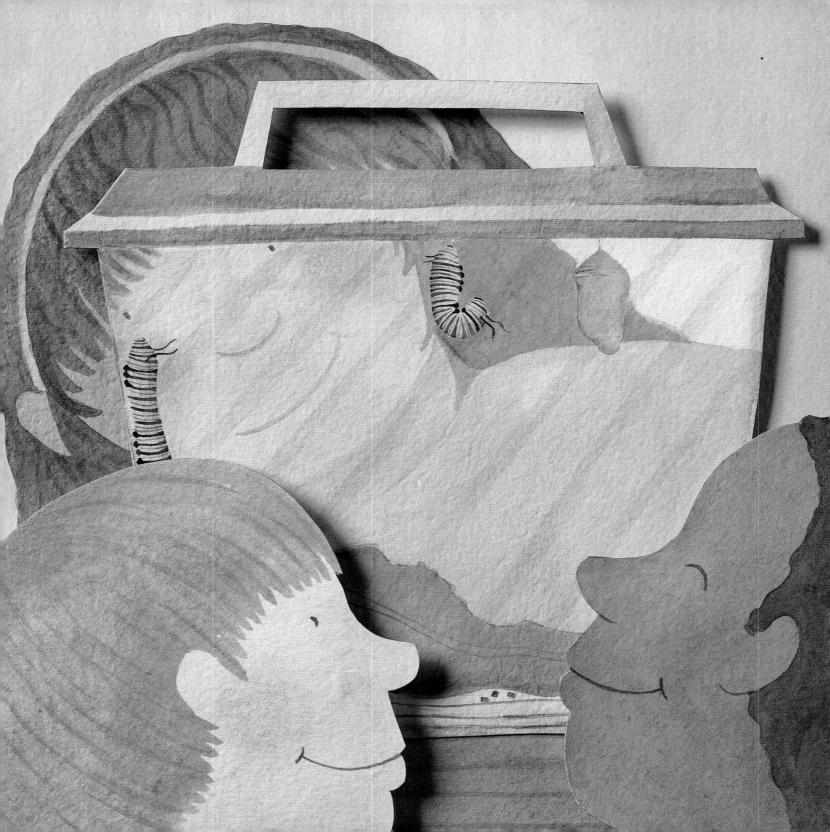

We watched the other caterpillars climb up the box
and hang in the shape of the letter J.
Their skins split, and each became
a green chrysalis with a ring of shining gold spots.

For ten days they hung there.
They didn't eat. They didn't move.
"I wish they'd do something," said Julianna.
"They *are* doing something," I said.
"They're becoming butterflies."

Chrysalises becoming butterflies

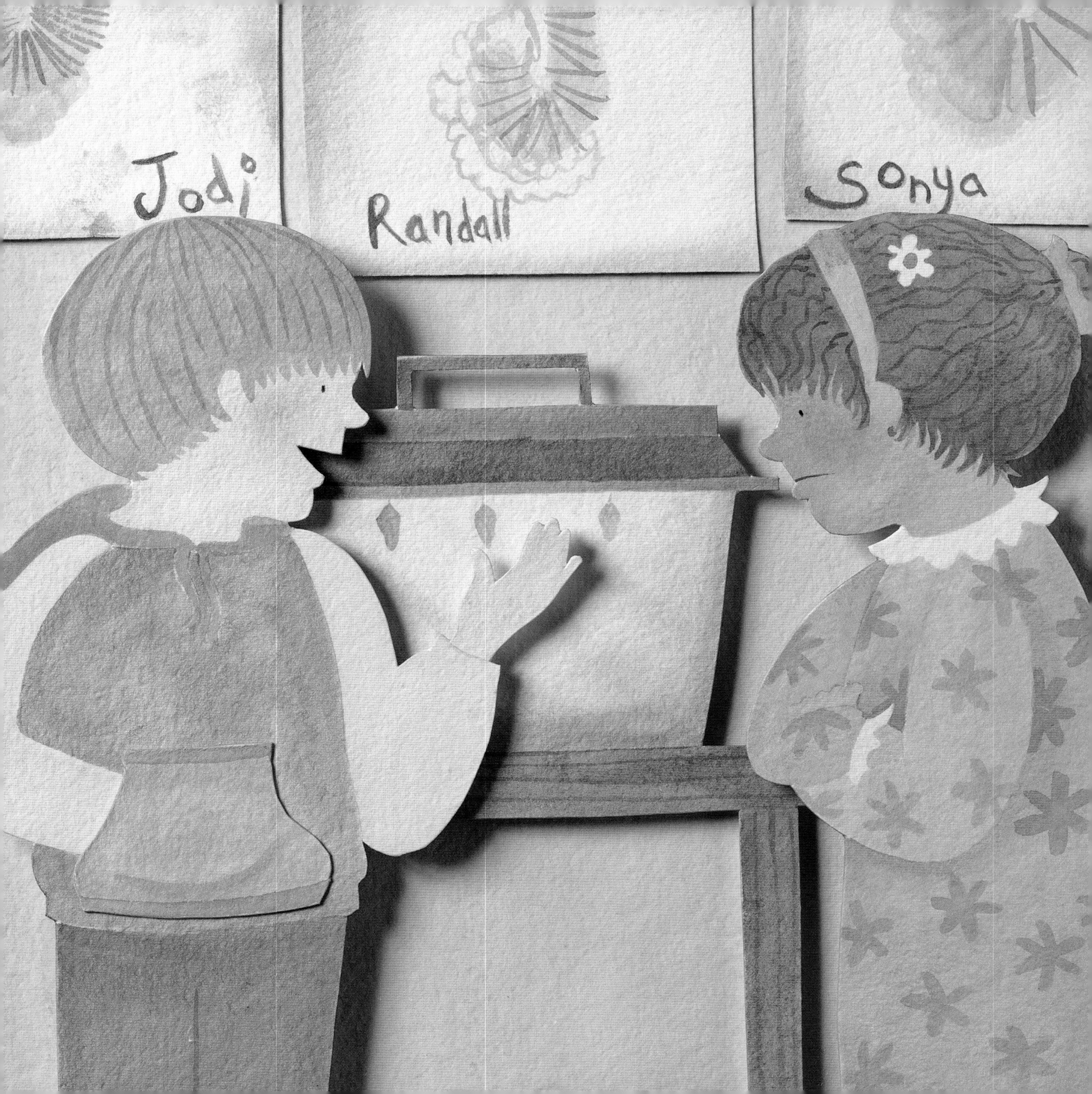
Jodi
Randall
Sonya

One morning a chrysalis turned dark brown.
"What's wrong?" I cried.
"Nothing is wrong. But now it's time," said Miss Dana.
"It's almost a butterfly. You'll see."

The darkened chrysalis

We watched as the shell of the chrysalis peeled away.
It had turned clear as glass.
A butterfly with wet and folded wings hung from it,
waiting for its wings to dry.
"Wow!" everyone said. "Look at that!"

The shell of
the chrysalis

That afternoon we drew pictures of our beautiful butterflies.
When their wings were dry we opened the window.
Each one sipped nectar from the flowers outside,
then fluttered up to the sky.
"But I wanted them to stay!"
Julianna looked very sad.

The butterfly sips nectar from a coneflower.

Goodbye,
butterflies.

"They'll sip nectar all summer," Miss Dana said.
"But they'll fly far south before winter comes.
Butterflies can only live when the weather is warm."
On the map, she showed us a place in Mexico.
"This is where they will go," she said.
We wrote a letter to the boys and girls
at a school in Chincua, Mexico.
"Please take good care of our butterflies," we said.

Mexico on the globe

United States of America

Mexico

Central
America

One cold winter day we got a letter back from
the boys and girls at the school in Mexico.
They sent us a picture of a tree covered with butterflies.
All of us looked and looked, wondering which
were the three butterflies we hatched in our classroom
and set free to fly so far away.

The letter
from Mexico

Dear Miss Dana's Class,
Here is a photograph
of butterflies on a tree.
Maybe your butterflies
are here.

Just some of the millions of butterflies
that gather in Mexico

AUTHOR'S NOTE

The butterflies in this story are Monarch butterflies. Their caterpillars eat nothing but milkweed leaves, so a female Monarch must lay her eggs on milkweed plants.

The eggs hatch into tiny caterpillars. Each sheds its skin five times, over a period of two to three weeks. The period between sheddings is called an

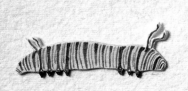

"instar." The time of each instar varies, depending on how warm the weather is. When a caterpillar reaches its fifth instar it is ready to become a chrysalis (kri-sah-lis). Some people mistakenly call a chrysalis a cocoon, but a cocoon is covered with layers of silk thread. Only moths make cocoons.

In the wild, butterflies go through their metamorphosis in the summer and begin their migration south to Mexico in early fall. (The California Monarch, however, doesn't migrate to Mexico, because the weather doesn't turn too cold for it to survive.) A Web site that tells a great deal more about Monarchs is: www.MonarchWatch.org or you can E-mail them at monarch@ukans.edu.

Monarchs are only one of many kinds of butterflies around us. There are pictures of other butterflies, with each one's caterpillar, on the endpapers of this book. How many have you seen?

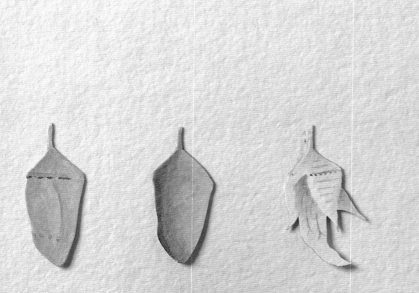

ACKNOWLEDGMENT

With thanks to Cindy Hepp of Milkweed Café (www.milkweedcafe.com) in Pinckneyville, Illinois, for all her help

Text copyright © 2002 by Anne Rockwell
Illustrations copyright © 2002 by Megan Halsey

First published in the United States of America in 2002 by Walker Publishing Company, Inc.

Published simultaneously in Canada by Fitzhenry and Whiteside, Markham, Ontario L3R 4T8

For information about permission to reproduce selections from this book, write to Permissions, Walker & Company, 435 Hudson Street, New York, New York 10014

Library of Congress Cataloging-in-Publication Data

Rockwell, Anne F.
    Becoming butterflies / by Anne Rockwell ; pictures by Megan Halsey.
        p. cm.
    Summary: A class observes the various stages caterpillars go through to become butterflies.
    ISBN 0-8027-8797-5 (hardcover)
    --ISBN 0-8027-8798-3 (reinforced)
1. Butterflies--Metamorphosis--Juvenile literature. [1. Caterpillars.
2. Butterflies 3. Metamorphosis.] I. Halsey, Megan, ill. II. Title.

QL544.2 .R635 2001
595.78'9--dc21   2001026935

The illustrations for this book were first painted in watercolor on Passion watercolor paper, then individually cut out and glued in layers to create a three-dimensional piece of art.

Photograph on page 29 © Kathy Adams Clark.

Book design by Diane Hobbing/SNAP-HAUS GRAPHICS

Printed in Hong Kong
10 9 8 7 6 5 4 3 2

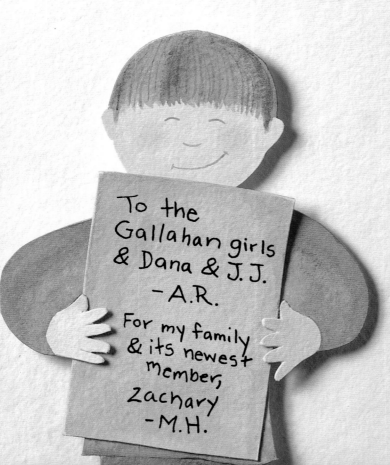

To the Gallahan girls & Dana & J.J.
   —A.R.

For my family & its newest member, Zachary
   —M.H.

Eastern Tiger Swallowtail
(Papilio glaucus)

Buckeye
(Junonia coenia)

Silvery Blue
(Glaucopsyche lygdamus)

Snout
(Libytheana bachmanii)

Red Admiral
(Vanessa atalanta)